prodigal
selves

prodigal
selves

Poems by Jeremy Fulwiler

EVANS
CREEK
PRESS

Evans Creek Press
24330 Lahser Road
Southfield, MI 48033

www.evanscreekpress.com

Thank you, Tatianah Thunberg, for the cover photo at Lake Michigan.

Thank you, Colleen Neuman, of [coll.neu] photography, for the photo of the author.

Photo on page 89 by the author at Dover Stone Church, Dover Plains, NY

ISBN: 978-0-9986700-0-3

to my prodigal selves

& to those who help me welcome them home,
especially Sabin

table of contents

prodigal selves

& other people

invitation

faith

preface

My life greatly expanded both inward and outward over the past five years, the years during which these journal entries had been written and revised. As I connected more deeply with the lost parts of myself, I found myself connecting much more deeply with others. These poems are windows into this mindbody growth journey and have also been some of my medicine along the way.

I am deeply grateful to those, too many to mention, who have helped steward me into and along my own mindbody healing journey. And grateful to those who now give me their trust, so that I may help steward theirs.

A few readers engaged in a responsive process with me during the compiling of this volume; some of whom also offered literary support. Receiving their candid and expressive reactions gave me a sense of being accompanied in the otherwise solo experience of revising my journaled poetry for publication. I know it also enriched the book. Thank you Rod Santos, Annie Brown, Valerie Linet, Lori Lichtman, Erin Stohl, Mark Snyder, Michele Allen, and Amy Knag for your caring and extensive responses. Others rooted me on after they reviewed a draft: thank you Deborah Werner, Sarah Insel, Michael Peters, Heather Brown, Melissa Butler, Beth Gartland and Amy Peirano Derksen. What a gift to receive you all in this way!

To your wellness beyond words…

J.F.
Ferndale, Michigan

prodigal
selves

prodigal selves

i welcome you
i welcome you all
all of me from every day
every day of pain
and confusion
every day of curiosity
pleasure
love
and enrapturement
every day of hatred
greed
recklessness
and rage
i welcome you from every day there ever was
every day that is today
and every day that ever there will be
open arms
no questions asked
no rationale required
i am here
infinitely
for you
all of me from every single day

there is room
for us all

meditation

uncoiling the false ribs wrapped around my chest

while holding myself in a gentle steady light

i shift my mind like a parent cradling a newborn –

in slow responsive awe

battle cry

tending moments quiet enough
where i can feel the tightness coming on
where i can hear the clank
of the dull bronze armor being hooked
in place

        just under my skin

        preparing me for a battle

        that no longer exists

plates of armor nearly everywhere
so thin i almost don't notice
unless i tend moments quiet enough
where i can hear the clank

and watch
as my light begins
to close in
on itself

i can hold you differently

and so it was that i felt the terror
of betraying myself

the internal industry of war

      decades of battles cutting into my ground
      buried fast with putrid mud
      and covered over with sod and hedges

i didn't even know that i was forgetting
those old distant fields

but i did a good job
i strangely treasured the ignorance
though finally
it just cost too much
this forgetting cost the best of me

the unknown

and unmarked

best

      but i have been preparing for you

rise up

reach out

be felt in your rich resonance!

my heart is ready for this sorrow

i can hold you differently

i can feel you now

i can honor the fallen

they shall be born again

tsunami

my personal meteorology has a rich history including
at least one tsunami

water had been pulled out to sea all right
for decades that felt like minutes
Ocean Wisdom had been kind to me:
when i couldn't stand strong enough
in the daily surf
she pulled out
and out
back
far

and collected

then
later
minding my
own business
i began taking baths
and then, for months, prayed
i prayed in domestic salt water
as it drained out i prayed it would
let me feel what i feared feeling, i prayed
for Ocean Wisdom to cease holding back the surf

and she did

without much warning
she released

                        i was pulverized

the velocity of water
split me at the cells
all scattered in an instant
to reanimate the myriad dead

now and again
i find them walking out of the water
lost & found & very alive

august morning

today i felt him reach for me
his little hands
   browned by the summer sun
reached through the veils of humidity & time

finger tips to finger tips
we touched
then palm to palm
and then i was fully holding him
   this little wizard
   whose wonder finally found an audience
   that could receive him

and the audience of me
   finally reunited
   with the magic
   i lost decades ago
   while trying to play baseball
   with the other boys

as a thousand fluttering leaves

or "why did i want to cut this poem? i must have been afraid of something"

wild
green
unknown
plants
growing on the other side
of the window

only now the glass has disappeared
and

        loamy moss
        coarse crisp leaves
        and smooth stems
        summon me

foliage that would usually scare me in such quantity
now captivates
no lattice to give it boundary
no window to hold it at bay
i let it grow close
       even around me
until i too am wilderness

i give over
  am grown over
and feel
  as a thousand fluttering leaves
in the wind

portal

how full
how full it is – my mended body
as i unfold the past before me
boxes unloaded
        contents fanned out

the graffiti of my story

my hero's journey – oh you brave child! – into adulthood
tassels and banners and photos
        and birthday cards from my heroes
        – the beloveds passed on – with x's
        & o's so real i can feel them
        against my skin

        as i feel the crossing over
                between grief & gratitude
        resting at the summit
                between the two

viewing the kingdom of my life
i breathe in this air
this strange air!
both fresh & musty
whirling around me
        or – it's dancing – beckoning
yes
yes!
i dance with the forgotten

the stored away
to the soundtracks etched in my ear

eventually to settle down the mountain
and rest again squarely
where i dot this i

red tree

my eye is drawn
    to the red tree in the center
there are acres of foothills
    surrounding the valley
and still my eye is drawn
    to the red tree in the center

yet it disappears
when i receive the whole vision before me
miles of thousands of trees
                of lives
                of generations
                of infinite stories though the village is
                      small
                layers of history – interwoven

miles of many years of my own life
      kept safe
      kept as ghosts within these trees
      years of wonder
      years of discovering me through these hills

              there i am now

i
the red tree in the center
who disappears
                    completely
when received
whole vision

one of those rare days

This poem uses the Humanistic pronouns hu/hum (pronounced hyoo/hyoom) in place of gendered pronouns (i.e. she/her, he/him).

i became aware of someone screaming
screaming for life
deep in my chest

i did not try to shut hum up

today instead
i began by listening to the screams
and then holding
                        with my awareness
the screaming one
a protected sphere where screaming
was ok
and i held this space
            and the screaming one within it
and reclined in the chair –
just witnessing

and i then became aware of how hard it would be for me
to continue holding this space
while interacting with others
that somehow when i'm with others
i contract a part of me

14

(
not enough room?
too ugly to share?
)

and become smaller

and my screaming one
frail
again
shoved into a dusty chest

- my chest -

and forgotten
for a while
until i'm quiet enough
to hear the screams
again

truth be told
i know this screaming one well
hu and i have spoken before
and there have been days
rare days
where i've held hum in my arms and mind quite a bit

settling into the needs and
deep fears and concerns of
a part of myself so abused
and neglected
so unwanted

that i keep trying to forget

(
really, i don't have to actively
try
to forget
i just do –
habit
)

but in the remembering
i change
however many dimensions existed before
suddenly there are more

many more

and as awful as it must seem to be with a screaming one
truly, there becomes a sweetness

a settling
a settling in
a return

a homecoming
a regeneration

and i feel more alive more ok more rest
even in motion
more rested
because i'm not holding down
a part of me

so vital

witness

cars whir outside in the cold
going to where they go

my breath whirs softly inside & out
finding me where

        my mind creeks

                and crunches

          and topples

      and rebuilds

                  and screams

      and wriggles

          and wob
             bles

     scrambles

              freaks the fuck out!
                  wreaks havoc

then hides

before busting out of
the closet screaming and flailing in some
crazy costume only a three-year old could
fathom

then exhausted
sinks down & sobs

i witness – hands open
speechless & breathing
slowly moving closer

molasses

the molasses
of my self

needs space
to breathe in

to take time in

to not feel
rushed in

to just be in

it relies on the other

parts of me

to give it shape

and to get out of
the way

and let it roll

real slow-like

in its own

good time

let it ride
and then

sink

deep beneath
the surface

to be stirred in

where it somehow

sweetens

everything

unfolding

it's like the fence disappeared
and heaven replaced it

little angels
         recently confined
now unfold their wings
in the light that simply is

oh to fly again!
if only for a moment
to be life-sized and alive

& other
people

emperor's new clothes

such thin lines are drawn
like the space between the furs
        on the back of a cat
or the outline of a leaf
        against the others on a tree
or the lines that remain on the face of a child
        for a fleeting moment after a smile

such thin lines
like the space between the threads
        woven in a bed sheet
or the outline of a ripple's crest
        against the rest of the lake
or the lines that remain in my memory
        just after waking from a dream

such thin lines exist
such thin lines
between me and you
where i have instead grown borders

and like the emperor's new clothes
i've worn them with pride
as if somehow i still needed more
than my own naked soul

after getting hung up on another life pattern, i pause

sinking slowly
like a leaf

sensation

returns to me

though currents toss

things about

the lake floor remains ready for touch

courtship

i step into you slowly
bid you fully receive all of me

i am in ecstasy
rocked by you
my whole body elevated
each caress
a soaring arc of pleasure

i am in my full strength
i have shown up to you willingly
i am all but naked
      your eager lover

all the while knowing
that your cloaked waters
could take me instantly
and never let go

you cleanse me
as easily
as you could kill me

wet feet

let metaphor fill my life
an ocean
filling the air
every movement, a stroke of intention
every breath, visible as bubbles

my otherwise invisible reality would be
suddenly palpable
shareable
other experienceable

      i'm not crazy – see!

"no jeremy, you're not crazy
we see it now
we see you now
how did you ever put up with us before?"

well, i would just swim in the ocean
and then come to your door
with wet feet

an open letter to vulnerability

you point the
way to my
deepest
long-
ing

you

the
angel
leading
me through
this soft pain

will you

marry me?
in tears and on bended knee
i ask

earlier that morning we took a walk
a growing pressure
a five year pregnancy
kicking inside my heart
but despite the probability
it wasn't yet time

as we approached the car to leave
would you say my water broke?
i couldn't take a step further away from the creek
the air before me was too
dense
or would you say it was too empty?

simply
i stopped
my body
couldn't
go forward
like this

and i asked him to go on another walk

so we turned around

and walked in silence
the sun had now come up over the trees
dry cushions appeared on a bench

this is the place in time
sky reflecting in the water
contractions quicken
while new life
Demands Itself and

i hear it
he hears me
i hear him

Yes

and just like that
there are three
of us

up like a ribbon and out like a river

my pelvis & heart
open

      and beautiful streamings emerge
                flowing up like a ribbon
         and out like a river

at once
such vast peace
and such deep sadness

feast of heaven & hell

i feel my sadness
for how wonderful life is
how miraculous and fleeting
this feast of heaven & hell is presented
for the taking

pockets of memories
    feel soft and warm
    willing my hand to enter and rest
        my cells expand
          some part of me deep inside surrenders

meanwhile
it is today
love in the shape of my husband
light in the shape of the sun
belonging in the shape of a home

such bounty

this place & time
a rolling feast
and i,
        so
        very
        hungry

friday afternoon, summer

we are floating

   in a ring
    our rafts tethered together by warm hands
    & ankles
   pulses moving through ripples of body
  & water

 the breeze pulls us across
 to the edge where tall grass and
lily pads tickle us and

we feel land-locked.

away!
 start the motor!
  (a.k.a. erin's hands & arms
   pulling us back across with surprising
   umph as the rest of us feel rich)

  and we are queens and kings
   of lake, life & found families
    grateful that at least 5 out of 6
     rafts aren't leaking
     and that we have hat brims to rest our eyes

    this is not just one
    day
    but several scattered across summers, homes

diagnoses, buildings, breakups near & far
new loves, weddings, books
questions, answers, questions, no answers
water
cool
air
hot
we
love
we
love
we
love
back to the edge
again already!
(the breeze is swift)
we shove away from the shoreline and

i dive in
my turn to be the motor
i push one raft while kicking in the water
and slowly
we all start to move

feel rich my friends

float
on
air

skipping stones

this saturday afternoon i shared
with him one of the memories of my own
childhood

                  someone taught me how
             but i don't remember who
          Cumberland Lake
           the point of a cove
        clay and slate everywhere
          stones to fit any hand
            perfect for skipping over the
            deep wet serpentine
               wilderness

he never had before
and this day
even though Detroit River's stones are
not nearly so ideal for skipping
i teach him

we will both remember

standing along the rocky shore
 the waves lap up surprisingly
   and pump out through our heart valves
as we and the stones do our best

i still feel the water
cold at my feet
and full of sun from light
years away

over half his life
he has become my
part-brother part-nephew part-son part-friend
and more than the sum

this is a day that fills
me with knowing:
      everything that came before
      was worth it

      at least for me

even if
at best
we could only make three skips

in
  a
    row

      we have earned each other

sidewalk symphony

watching people negotiate space
on the sidewalk
    going

        going

            sometimes looking

                    gone

we have no idea
    do we?
of what our bodies are saying
our faces
our footsteps and strides
our gasping
    reaching

        onwards   tumble

we may put on our clothes
and choose them with great deliberation
to express ourselves
    but they are merely static
    against the striking statements
    made
        by the height of our shoulders
        the rhythm of gait
        the holding of our head
        the line cut by our body
        moving

        through

space

mostly i just notice the static myself
but not right now
not while digesting tabbouleh after a heavenly massage

now
i notice the symphony of meaning
       resonating down the channel
       of a sidewalk
       on a sunny afternoon

... in bed

Words sometimes informally added to the end of the message in a fortune cookie for amusement. Here's mine: "You will live a good life."

in bed
when, just tired
we feel for each other's hand
a final gesture of the day
from any angle
temperature
temperament
   or
     configuration

it doesn't matter

his skin my skin our skin
   the plane of contact
     reorganizes my stubborn cells
   welcomed and welcoming –
    i am changed

instantly

a good life indeed

invitation

invitation

do less tension
is the invitation

no expectation to do more
 of anything

not even to relax
  simply to do less
of tension

it's like one less thing to do every day hour moment

-     but somehow
-     it has gotten easier
-     to add things
-     to the invisible
-     to-do list

than it has to take the unserving things

away

and make room

by not adding

the unneeded

do less tension

is the invitation…

...begin anywhere

moon pull

blues greens oceans of life
        lapping up at my feet
rhythms rolling out
        over & over again
not mastered by any musician
        just free in their power

alive! alive!
swellingly alive energy stretched by a little rock in the sky

        oceans move
        grounds swell
        skies unleash
        pole to pole
        our bodies too, little planets
        of ocean/ground/sky
            shift

complete vulnerability to the pull of the moon

saying no is futile
ignoring is temporary
diving in is a celebration

i will still fit in this body
        at the high tide of pleasure
i will still fit in this body
        at the low tide of pain

i can still fit in this body
    if i insist

    or
    i can
    surrender my skin

courtship II

i asked her if i could be her lover
she was loud & impassioned –
        as a forceful moving mountain range

i waited

and still she said nothing to me
i moved into her a bit

      still nothing

i waded

      still nothing

i felt for her boundaries
      naked in my intention

          and then
              consent!

i plunged in head first
wet & satisfied
      i rolled around in her
      knowing she was the one on top
      yielding to me only insomuch as
      i would yield to her

she exhausted & delighted me
       challenged & emboldened me
         humbled & exulted me

i wanted more
but could take little more
and had little else to give
       save only for the energy to return to shore
       and dripping
       look back on her abundance

loosening up

watching myself get caught up in getting caught up
witnessing my concern with being concerned
feeling the clench of fearing my clench

i invite ease
  to roll over me easily
to roll through my lungs
   and settle in my eyes
         my belly
         my feet
and all the other nooks, corners & crannies

and i invite ease
to permeate what i think of as my border

     today
     i rest
     on
     my breath

and grow fuzzy
in the distinctions of my obsessions

i expand

    a little

        into the barrier zone

between me and Everything Else
loosening the belt buckles worn
over my senses

   and let

   myself

     receive

even on vacation

releasing the clench
one reminder at a time
the negotiation
      between
  holding on for dear life
and

      letting

            go

        for

    d

     e

    a

     r

    l
  i

    f

  e

it is hard to remember that the tight grip

is not my true shape
>tummy turning in on itself
>legs stiff as wood
>back braced from the inside out
>jaw set
>eyes fixed
>brain angular

this is a picture of someone else
>(perhaps)
but not me
not *really*
not me in the light of today

>perhaps me frozen in the distant past
>or me on a bad vacation
>>(which this certainly is not)

no

i am something altogether different

>>>>i
>>>>breathe

from the narrow summit

*This poem uses the Humanistic pronouns hu/ hum (pronounced
hyoo/ hyoom) in place of gendered pronouns (i.e. she/ her, he/ him).*

                              up
                        up
i felt my energy go up

                                and get stuck
                          somewhere around
                              my shoulders neck &
                                        head
                              and that's where i lived

    spoke

    felt

    and feared

    and laughed

    and thought
                    way up there
                    in that little
                      space

it was like i got smaller
and like in the movies
my voice got higher
i breathed little breaths

at the narrow summit of my lungs

and very little

      dropped

    down

very
little

into a deeper place of me
a fuller place
a very big place
      a very powerful place

even still, i had fun
but the "i" who had fun was also very little
i can't say very much *quantity* of me had fun
    the large portion "left over"
    was lonely

i'm with hum today
and hu's glad i'm back

and though something about what happened is cute on
the
outside

it is not cute on the inside
it feels like i'm slowly suffocating
and the closer i get to the "what" which
is suffocating
the sadder the truth is
the sadder i feel

i lose the best of me

for helium

but

i can
in fact
breathe

further

down

deeper in the place

the part

that needs oxygen

to survive

that very big place
basin of fire & water

breathing does the darnedest things

letting air fill me

                stretching me out to the
                    edges of what i thought i was
                filling in the gaps & voids &
                numbness

revealing sensations of pain, tingles & lightness

                    expanding me from a
                narrow space out
                  into the atmosphere

waking from an amnesia of limitation

                    from the crinkled
                      wrappers left behind

rising from the tiredness of holding so much back

                    into the return of
                contact –
            my skin ready & willing
        to touch & be touched
     even amidst the parts of me
not yet thawed

reminded

light
water
foam
salted air
reflected sparkles
moving always
dissolving always
reenergizing always
the sound
the pounding
the sand
carved & reshaped
like my world
like my possibilities
like my movement
nothing here is rigid
and i am reminded
that my attempts elsewhere to make it so
are futile

arcs

drops of last night's rain
  still hang on the jade plant
   little arcs of light
    drawn into the drops
     like jewels taking a sip of nectar
     so much light on this cloudy summer morning
    so much life hanging on
even as autumn begins to whisper a greeting

      i hear it
       i too am bent in the light
       held in a drop of water
        i too am sipping the nectar of morning
        cradled in an arc
       i am just now learning
       how

again & again & again

cold on my nose
3 bird chirps
writing a poem
the bird chirps again
and again
traffic flows in the distance like a rushing river
i feel tension enter my shoulders
and choose to release it
it happens again, the tension
and i release it again
this time along with my jaw

ahhhhhh good

crickets, several
making their own chirps
sunlight finding its way from the tallest branches
now down to our garage
soon, even the dappled willow will be wet with light

morning comes in early September
as the kids return to school
morning takes its time getting ready
until finally it just is
and i release the tension in my shoulders again

rest

over lettuce wraps
we discussed rest
and the difference between

    resting to do… (so that i can go back to work
    refreshed tomorrow, or have the energy to go out
    tonight, so that i can get better when i'm sick)
    …those things

and we also discussed

    resting to rest…

    (for the pleasure of rest

        because it feels good

       because it's so damn natural

     because it leaves space to be

       space to be in bliss

     or not – space to be just as

    just as i am
          right

             now

because being is a miracle
no one else can construct

because being alive is a miracle
   no one can guarantee

because breathing is a miracle of massaging
my life from the inside
       out
    sending
      ripples
  of vitality
      around
      at a rhythm uniquely this)

…we discussed that kind of rest as well

and didn't finish the food

 we felt full

and brought the rest home

life good true

this mid-morning
resting in nature
feels too
      simple too
            beautiful too
                  possible too
                        expanded

to be real

and yet

this breeze is
      real this sun is
            real these flowers are
                  real this breath and skin are
                        real this time

now

is real

this is my life
river run anew
carrying a message barely decipherable in words

life
  good
    true

dance

a day of freedom
my Self revealing secrets to me:

desperation can dissolve into delight
        tight grips do give way to
        thoughts walking lightly through the park
        sunlight streaming through
            hands ears lips and feet

no need to hold down the cellar doors dorothy!
let 'em flap
let the wind carry you away
landing in oz
already knowing how to click your heels
3 times 4 times 5 times 6
               times to the beat

of the naked drummer

carrying the yellow rose

faith

faith

each step really holds the ocean in it

they are my own eyes that deceive me
when all i see is land

little glass of water

returning to mother ocean
waves crashing in my ears
my own rhythm being massaged to a slower pace
receiving the message of satisfaction
      the message of relinquishing
          of pouring
              myself
                  into my life
   a little glass of water
   into an infinite basin
   without a fight
   as water laps the shore
   stretching out what has been inspired

sacrament

wading in the water
well above my waist
gentle ocean hands
hold me up in the waves

    as if suspended

      timeless in time

      spaceless in space

held
moved
  this way & that
up & down
  with ever so little effort
even

  can

     float

part of me
just wet
and another
baptized

ground hold

whether slate
grass
mud, moss, concrete

    ground

this gym shoe translates
sandals translate
the ends of the nerves on the soles of my feet
translate this language between ground & gravity

      so held
      i am so held
          so nestled
      in this little sliver of green
      cradled between towers

      i am so held
          so nestled
      in this little sliver of time
      cradled between breakfast & the Next Thing

      i am so held
          so nestled
      on this little spinning ball
      though it hurtles through space!

i am held

to where i belong
this earthen bed

i am

all the time

held

morehere

another world
where the curtains turn sheer
mono turns stereo
my hands are tender & ungloved
my voice comes from someplace below
and my feet become living bridges from ground to flesh

not because i am anywhere other
than where i usually am
just because i am more here

losing the rope

so i'm deep in the forest
at the well i'd been looking for
thirst coming on for plainly too long
my skin stained with sweat & dirt
a shallow sweetness rising from the dry ground

i am here
at the well
thirsty as hell

i start pulling up the water bucket
then i drop the rope
i hear the bucket splash
as if it's in a dream
i try again reaching half-
heartedly
i see the rope in front of me
or do i?
one moment double vision
next moment nothing
i know all i need to do is reach for it again and
start pulling
right?
      but
             i'm
        just
           too distracted
                by
           the

                    what?
               is it the light?
               or shadow?
               my hunger?
               that sound?

i don't know

i'm just here in the forest
thirsty and confused
i want to leave and go home
but i know i can do this
i know i can pull the rope again
i know i can drink here
i know it in my bones – and deeper

even still
i have lost the rope
i cannot find the rope

i step back
with a mouth that hurts
and forget i'm even thirsty

what to do when having lost the rope

in stillness
remember water –

let remembering
move me

rainbow drops

with my eyes mostly closed
the sun makes rainbow drops through my lashes
this has happened many times before
but this morning is the first time i looked

i am humbled
the slower i move, the more i receive
gone is my pride in Fast
after all those years of habitual wing-like rapidity

even this morning
sniffles & sneezes & all
the light wakes up my body's best attempt at chloroform
earthing the rooted tree in me

while spider webs glisten neon indigo & blue in the light
ready to receive the rapid flying by

response to the last poem

but sometimes i do choose fastness
i shower in it
light up in it
find myself
      my chutzpah
              in it

  amen
 amen
  amen

times to reach deep
and run like hell
      reveling in it

           arms wide & bat-shit crazy

    reflecting sunlight
    & casting shadows everywhere

birdsongs

listening to morning birdsongs change across the season
while watching different perennials bloom in sequence
different textures for ears
                              eyes

a massage for my senses measured not in minutes
                              but months

and if i dare feel these morning touches?

                    sing my life
                    with the unabashed spontaneity
                    of a robin
                    perched
                    in the light
                    of sunrise

the Whole Sound

at times like this moment here

it's as if my ears soften

into large spirals

of fragile life forms

simply expanding out from incidental ocean

depths

undefended from the rush of noise

breaking from the waves above

receiving many sudden sounds

and also deeper swells of vibration
at first soundless

and then suddenly present
audible
eternal

one ocean

body alchemy

watching it happen
in real time

my body changes
      thought-to-thought
      movement-to-movement
      breath-by-breath
like the weather
         but faster
         like a spell
         some type of magic spell

         think the words
         or shift my shape

      and the universe changes

with just the slightest tilt of my bodymind

         presto

         alchemy

         rust-to-gold

      possibility
      turns inside out

make a doorway appear

   where before stood only a wall

call it science
call it faith
call it magic
for heaven's sake call it something!

it is ours to learn
ours to master

it seems so subtle – it's hard to be patient
to some it seems invisible – hard to believe
to me it's flat-out real-life – body alchemy

birthday

oh how softly happy i am
such simplicity

in this body to which i was birthed, i feel.

i get to feel

        breezes
        heart aches
        beats
        and chocolate pleasures
        and fears
        discomforts
        warm water
        my sweetheart's skin
        loneliness
        and salt on my lips

all signs
all signs pointing this way & that
as i navigate this brave new world
of every moment

believe!
believe – for It (that thing
i've been waiting for) –
is here now

i would say "how lucky!"

but it's simply my birthright

the "luck" is that somehow
i'm aware that it's not luck
not chance

just available
everyday

time to go

and then it was time to go

    the dogs barking
    the fresh blacktop in the sun
    the shoulder of the road covered
        with worms in varying stages of decay
    and the slat of tension
        running diagonally across my eyes
    all saying:
    enough

i had been invited back
    grateful for this time – not stolen
but like a hot day in october
it only lasts so long…

now finished

like my favorite tree
a once sheltering sycamore struck by lightning
again
another half itself broken off
again
and the rest of it this time
resigned

now

there

place of countless prayers & journeys

light can finally reach the saplings

stone church

water
has worked its way
through this giant stone
and created a haven within

unleashing a labyrinth of sound
working its way through
the labyrinth of molecules
within me

      may i be carved
      by this music
      of stone water & gravity!

      that all that is extra
            be washed away

      that

         as a haven within

               i emerge

author's note

Thanks for joining me in this experience. If you'd like to share any personal or expressive reactions of your own to these pieces, you can find me at jeremyfulwiler.com. There you can also join my email list for unpublished poems, information on future books and projects, as well as wellness-related tools. Lastly, if you would consider writing a review on amazon.com, goodreads.com or other places of interest, doing so would be a welcomed way to support this book and my future writing projects. These reviews really help authors, and also help books get into the hands of those who would most value them. To your wellness beyond words!

about the author

Jeremy Fulwiler is founder of Wellness Beyond Words, a body psychotherapy and expressive arts counseling practice near Detroit (wellnessbeyondwords.com). Jeremy began keeping a personal journal about 30 years ago, studied Creative Writing and Dance at Otterbein University, released a full-length CD of original contemporary folk music in 2002 (*Embracing This*), and later completed graduate studies in Social Work at Columbia University. A lover of nature, and particularly of bodies of water, Michigan has since become a wonderful home.

www.ingramcontent.com/pod-product-compliance
Lightning Source LLC
LaVergne TN
LVHW041200080426
835511LV00006B/682